FAMOUS ARTISTS

Jillian Powell

Wayland

Famous People

Famous Artists
Famous Campaigners for Change
Famous Explorers
Famous Inventors
Famous Musicians
Famous Scientists

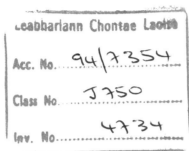
Picture acknowledgements
The publishers would like to thank the following for supplying pictures:
Archiv für Kunst und Geschichte, Berlin 5, 6, 7, 8, 9, 10, 13, 14, 15, 17, 18, 20, 21, 24, 25, 27, 29, 30, 32, 34, 35, 36, 38, 39, 43, 44; Bridgeman Art Library 16, 19, 41; Mary Evans Picture Library 11, 12, 19, 41; Topham *cover* (all), 37, 40, 42, 45; Julia Waterlow 28; Wayland Picture Library 4, 20, 31. *Les Demoiselles d'Avignon* by Pablo Picasso on page 38 appears by kind permission of the copyright holders © DACS, London 1993 and *Campbell's Soup Can I* by Andy Warhol, © Andy Warhol Foundation Inc. 1993.
Cover artwork by Peter Dennis.

Series and book editor: Rosemary Ashley
Series designer: Malcolm Walker

First published in 1993 by
Wayland (Publishers) Limited
61 Western Road, Hove
East Sussex, BN3 1JD, England

British Library Cataloguing in Publication Data
Powell, Jillian
   Famous Artists. -(Famous People Series)
   I. Title   II. Series
   709.2

ISBN 0-7502-0668-3

Typeset by Kudos Editorial and Design Services
Printed and bound in Italy by Rotolito Lombardo S.p.A, Milan

Contents

Leonardo da Vinci
'Renaissance Man' 4
Albrecht Dürer
Master print-maker 8
Michelangelo Buonarroti
Sculptor, painter and architect..11
Rembrandt van Rijn
Northern genius 15
Katsushika Hokusai
Master artist of 'the floating world' 19
Joseph Mallord William Turner
Master of 'coloured light' 22
Claude Monet
Leading Impressionist...26
Mary Cassatt
A woman painter in Paris 30
Vincent van Gogh
Tortured genius..33
Pablo Picasso
Twentieth-century genius 37
Barbara Hepworth
Sculptor of natural forms 40
Andy Warhol
Creator of Pop Art 43
Glossary...46
Books to read 47
Index 48

Introduction

Many artists have become famous by breaking new ground. They have experimented with techniques, using materials and methods in new and different ways, as Dürer did with print-making. They have changed the way we see things, as Monet did when he recorded his impressions of the world around him, and Picasso when he invented Cubism. These and other artists have changed the way we think about art, as Andy Warhol did with his concept of Pop Art. Often, they have been criticized for challenging the traditions of the art of their time. All the artists in this book broke new ground in the history of art.

Leonardo *da Vinci*

'Renaissance Man'

Leonardo symbolized the new ideals of the Italian Renaissance. He was a scientist as well as an artist, and he left thousands of drawings and notebooks filled with plans and ideas. His drawings include plans for a helicopter and a submarine, and he made studies of anatomy and of methods of flight, underwater diving and engineering. His most famous paintings include the *Mona Lisa* and his fresco of the *Last Supper*.

Leonardo drew this self-portrait when he was an old man.

In his wide-ranging interests and skills, Leonardo symbolized the great period of art and learning in Italy known as the Renaissance. He was a scientist as well as an artist, believing that artists need to understand how things work in order to paint them.

Leonardo was born in 1452, at Vinci in Tuscany, Italy. As a boy he loved animals, clothes and practical jokes! When he was fifteen he went to work for the artist Andrea del Verrocchio in Florence. Leonardo found himself in a busy workshop, working on portraits, sculpture, jewellery and costumes. Living in Florence, he was able to study works which marked a new beginning in Italian art, such as Ghiberti's bronze doors for the Baptistry church and Donatello's statue of David.

Leonardo became an amazingly skilled artist; a story says that Verrocchio gave up painting in despair when he saw how well his young pupil had painted the angel on the left in his master's picture *The Baptism of Christ*.

In 1472 Leonardo became a Master of the Painters' Guild of St Luke. His early works include the portrait *Ginevra de' Benci* (1474) and the *Adoration of the Kings*, which was

Leonardo's Last Supper *fresco shows Jesus Christ and His disciples eating together before He is betrayed by one of them.*

intended for an altarpiece for the monks of St Donato in Florence. In 1482 he went to work for Ludovico Sforza, Duke of Milan, introducing himself as a 'master and inventor of instruments of war'.

As court architect and engineer, his duties included supervising the construction and repair of buildings and advising on fortifications. He produced plans and studies for equipment such as bridges, scaling ladders, weapons and cannons. He also designed pageants and entertainments for the Duke, as well as making paintings and sculptures.

For one of his commissions, a bronze sculpture of Ludovico's father on horseback, Leonardo studied the anatomy of the horse, and made an 8-metre high clay model which he intended to cast in bronze. In the event, the Duke needed the bronze for cannons and the project was never completed.

It was while he was working at the court in Milan that Leonardo painted his famous *Last Supper* fresco at the convent of Santa Maria delle Grazie.

In 1499 French troops invaded Milan and Leonardo returned to Florence, where he worked as a military engineer for General Cesare Borgia. He also painted his famous portrait The *Mona Lisa*, showing his *sfumato* technique – a smoky effect of

The world's most famous portrait, the Mona Lisa. It is not known for sure who the sitter was, but she may have been the wife of a Florentine merchant.

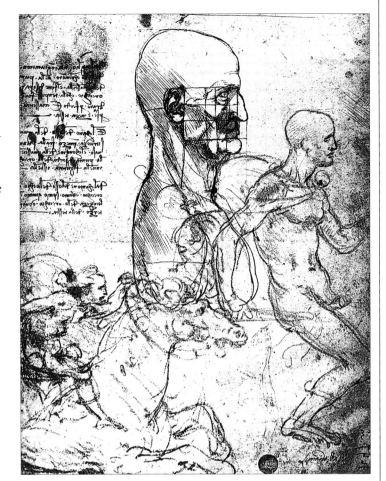

Leonardo filled sketchbooks with thousands of drawings. His mind ranged over a huge number of interests and his sketches include plans for scientific projects as well as drawings of humans and animals.

softly blended shadows which creates a sense of depth and atmosphere.

In 1506 Leonardo returned to Milan, now ruled by the French. He worked for King Louis XII of France, designing projects ranging from court entertainments to a canal system. In 1512 he moved to Rome, where he drew his self-portrait in red chalks, showing himself as an old man. Four years later he went to France, to work as painter, engineer and architect for King Francis I. He lived at a chateau near Amboise, where he died in 1519.

Leonardo left thousands of drawings and notebooks, mysteriously written in hand-writing which can only be read in a mirror. In many of these drawings he predicted much later discoveries and inventions, such as the circulation of the blood, and machines such as helicopters and submarines.

Dates

1452 born at Vinci, Tuscany, in Italy
1467 apprenticed to Verrocchio in Florence
1482 goes to Milan to work for Ludovico Sforza
1497 paints the *Last Supper*
1502-03 paints the *Mona Lisa*
1516 moves to France to work for King Francis I

Albrecht *Dürer*

Master print-maker

Albrecht Dürer was a master of print-making. He visited Italy and brought back many of the new ideas of the Renaissance to northern Europe. His paintings and drawings show the influence of Italian artists, and they greatly admired his work.

One of the earliest works we know by Albrecht Dürer is a self-portrait, drawn when he was only thirteen years old. The portrait shows how skilled he was, even at this early age, because he made it using a technique called silverpoint. This involved using an instrument with a silver wire tip on special white-coated paper. The technique does not allow for any corrections.

Dürer was born at Nuremberg in Germany in 1471. His father was a goldsmith and after a few years of schooling, Dürer began training in his workshop. He soon realized that he wanted to be an artist and he became an apprentice in the workshop of Michael

Dürer painted this view of his home town of Nuremberg. Wherever he was, at home or on his travels, he liked to draw or paint the scenery.

Wolmegut, who produced woodcut book illustrations.

In 1494 Dürer travelled south to Italy. The Italian landscape, especially the mountains and valleys he saw on his journey across the Alps, inspired him to paint rapid sketches in watercolour. Many of these sketches provided the background for later prints. Dürer was very impressed by the learning and lifestyle of Italian artists, compared to those living in Germany.

On his return, Dürer began to study mathematics, geometry and the work of Classical writers and artists. He set up his own workshop in Nuremberg and worked mainly on portraits and religious works. He also painted self-portraits which show him fashionably dressed like the important and well-established artists he had met in Italy.

It was during this period that Dürer became famous for his line drawings, with series such as the *Apocalypse*, a fourteen-page book of woodcuts illustrating the Book of Revelation from the Bible. In both his woodcuts and his engravings, Dürer used intricate techniques to give delicate effects of depth, light and shade.

In 1505 Dürer travelled to Italy again, where he met leading artists like Giovanni Bellini. Dürer's paintings and prints show how much he had been influenced by Italian ideas of art.

Dürer painted this self-portrait in 1498, after his first visit to Italy.

In turn, his prints were greatly admired in Italy, and in this way a link was formed between Renaissance Italy and northern Europe.

After his return to Germany, in 1512, Dürer became court painter to the Holy Roman Emperor Maximilian. His tasks ranged from illustrations for the Emperor's prayerbook to a huge print of a triumphal arch, three metres high!

In 1520 Dürer visited the Netherlands, recording the people he met and the landscapes and paintings he saw in a diary and sketchbook. On an unsuccessful trip to see a whale which had been stranded on a nearby beach, he caught a fever which left him in poor health for the rest of his life.

Dürer lived through the troubled years of the Counter-Reformation, and he knew and admired the Protestant reformers Martin Luther and Erasmus. At the time of his death, in 1528, he was writing a guide for young artists; setting out ideas about measurement, design for fortification, human proportion and art theory.

The Knight, Death and the Devil *is one of Dürer's most famous engravings.*

Dates

1471 born in Nuremberg, Germany	**1505** makes a second visit to Italy
1494 travels to Italy for the first time	**1512** becomes court painter to Emperor Maximilian
1497 publishes *Apocalypse* woodcuts	**1520** visits the Netherlands
	1528 dies

Michelangelo *Buonarroti*

Painter, sculptor and architect

Michelangelo was one of the greatest of the Renaissance artists. Although he regarded himself as a sculptor rather than a painter, his fresco painting covering the ceiling of the Sistine chapel in the Vatican in Rome is one of the world's greatest masterpieces of art. Near the end of his life, he designed the great dome for the Church of St Peter in Rome.

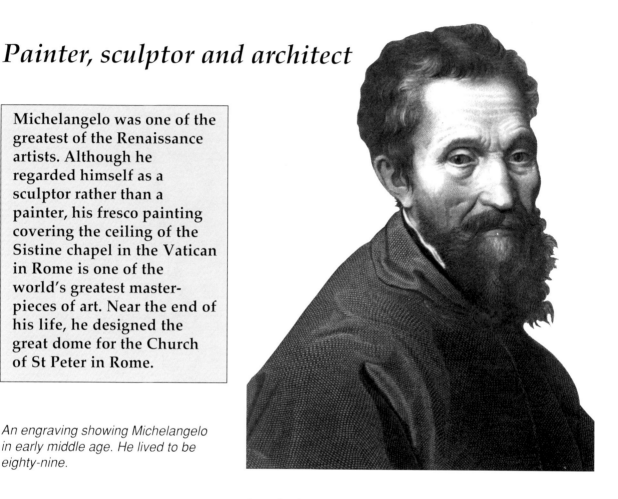

An engraving showing Michelangelo in early middle age. He lived to be eighty-nine.

Michelangelo's painted ceiling in the Sistine Chapel in Rome is one of the most famous paintings in the world, yet the artist always thought of himself as a sculptor. His extraordinary skills earned him the title 'the Divine Michelangelo', even in his own lifetime.

He was born in 1475 at Caprese, a small town south of Florence, where his father was the local governor. A few weeks after he was born, the family moved to Florence where, at the age of thirteen, Michelangelo went to work for the artist Domenico Ghirlandaio. In

Ghirlandaio's workshop, he learned the technique of fresco painting and made drawings from Classical sculpture.

After three years, Michelangelo transferred to the school for sculptors set up in the Medici gardens by Lorenzo de' Medici and supervised by the sculptor Bertoldo. His first copies of Classical sculpture in the gardens so impressed Lorenzo that Michelangelo was taken into his household to study art, music and poetry with the Medici children.

After Lorenzo died in 1492, Michelangelo travelled first to Bologna and then to Rome, where he won fame with his *Pietà* group, carved for a chapel in the great Church of St Peter. The sculpture of the Virgin Mary cradling the dead Jesus Christ, with its graceful pyramid shape and delicate carving, shows Michelangelo's immense skills as a sculptor.

In 1501, Michelangelo returned to Florence, where he was asked by the city rulers to carve a huge statue of David, taken from the story of David and Goliath in the Bible. This sculpture was to be a symbol of the city's freedom. It was carved from a block of marble over four metres high, in a specially-built shed, and was completed in 1504 and placed by the entrance to the Palazzo della Signoria in Florence.

The city of Florence as it was in Michelangelo's lifetime. The dome of Brunelleschi's cathedral and the tower of the Palazzo della Signoria dominate the skyline, as they do to this day.

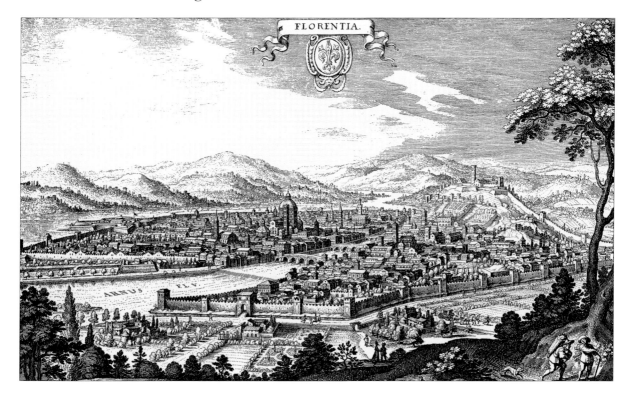

It took four days and forty men to move Michelangelo's giant statue of David to its position in the Piazza della Signoria, Florence. The original statue is now housed in a museum, and a replica stands in its place.

The following year, Michelangelo was called to Rome by Pope Julius II to begin work on a huge free-standing tomb with forty figures. The Pope kept altering the design for his tomb, and the project became, in Michelangelo's words, 'the tragedy of the tomb'.

In 1508, Pope Julius interrupted Michelangelo's work on the tomb because he wanted him to paint the ceiling of the Sistine Chapel in the Vatican. Single-handedly, working for over four years from scaffolding, Michelangelo painted the whole ceiling with over three hundred figures.

The Creation of Adam, *part of Michelangelo's painting of the Old Testament story that decorates the ceiling of the Sistine Chapel in Rome.*

After the Pope's death, in 1513, Michelangelo resumed work on the tomb, carving the giant figures of Moses and the Slaves. He also began work on the design for a new chapel at St Lorenzo in Florence, with memorials to the Medici family.

In 1523, the new Pope Paul III commissioned Michelangelo to paint a fresco of the *Last Judgement* on the altar wall of the Sistine Chapel. The subject of the painting reflected the new mood of uneasiness and fear of the people of Rome following the destruction and plundering of their city by the troops of the Holy Roman Emperor Charles V in 1527, and the troubled years of the Counter-Reformation which followed.

In his later years, Michelangelo was appointed chief architect to the new Church of St Peter and his design for its great dome was his last major project before he died at the age of eighty-nine in 1564.

Dates

1475 born at Caprese, near Florence
1496 moves to Rome where he carves the *Pietà*
1501 returns to Florence and carves statue of David
1505 called to Rome by the Pope to begin work on his tomb
1508 begins work on the ceiling of the Sistine Chapel
1564 dies

Rembrandt *van Rijn*

Northern genius

Rembrandt's self-portraits alone make him one of the greatest artists of all time. In these paintings, and other portraits, he was able to capture the mood and feeling of the sitter, with soft tones of light and shadow. He brought these qualities to all his paintings and etchings. Rembrandt transformed Dutch portrait painting, replacing stiff dull pictures with lively and dramatic group scenes. He also painted exciting scenes from the Bible and from history.

Few artists have left us as complete a record of their changing moods and feelings as Rembrandt. His enormous output included sixty self-portraits, showing his progress from an ambitious young artist to a thoughtful and world-weary old man, who had enjoyed success and also suffered loss and tragedy, throughout his life.

Rembrandt was born in Leiden in Holland in 1606, the son of a miller. He studied at the grammar school, then briefly at Leiden University, before beginning an apprentice-ship with a local artist. In 1624, he went to Amsterdam, to complete his training with a painter called Pieter Lastman. Lastman had

Rembrandt lived in the prosperous seaport of Amsterdam. This picture of the town was painted by a Dutch artist about the time Rembrandt was living there.

been to Italy and had studied the work of great Italian artists such as Caravaggio. In Lastman's workshop, Rembrandt painted subjects from the Bible and from history, and learned to master the effects of *chiaroscuro*, the balance of light and shadow in a picture.

In 1625, Rembrandt returned to Leiden and set up his own studio. He used local farmers, tradesmen and members of his own family as models; they posed in costume for his paintings of wise men, saints and apostles. He also produced etchings, often very tiny, but showing his mastery of the effects of depth, light and shade. Unusually for artists

Jacob blessing the children of Joseph. *Rembrandt painted this scene from the Bible in 1656. It shows the story of Joseph's sons being blessed by their dying grandfather.*

at this time, Rembrandt's subjects were often poor people, seen on the streets of Leiden.

In 1631, Rembrandt moved back to Amsterdam, which was then an important seaport. Here he obtained regular commissions for portraits from the wealthy citizens of the town. His group portrait of the Amsterdam Guild of Surgeons, the *Anatomy Lesson of Dr Tulp*, won him recognition in 1632, and other commissions for paintings soon followed.

In 1634, Rembrandt married Saskia van Uylenborch, the daughter of a picture dealer in whose house he had been living. Saskia brought him a large dowry and they moved into a town house in Amsterdam. Rembrandt painted his new wife many times, including pictures of them both dressed in exotic costumes, which he began collecting along with paintings, prints, jewellery and other works of art.

After twelve years of marriage, Saskia died, leaving a son, Titus. The same year, Rembrandt painted his famous *Nightwatch*, a group portrait of a volunteer civic guard which had been enlisted to defend Amsterdam in case of attack. In this painting, Rembrandt did not use the usual stiff, formal poses of most Dutch portraits of the time. Instead, he painted a busy crowd scene, alive with movement, light and colour.

In the following years, Rembrandt continued to paint scenes from the Bible as well as portraits, but Dutch tastes were changing and people were becoming less interested in buying religious works. Rembrandt's extravagant lifestyle, together with the declining popularity of his work, led to his bankruptcy in 1656. He had to give up

A small pen-and-ink self-portrait, showing Rembrandt in his studio clothes.

his house and all his possessions, but during this difficult period he was helped by his mistress, Hendrickje Stoffels, and by his son Titus. Sadly, in 1663, Hendrickje died, and Titus's death followed a few years later.

Throughout his life, Rembrandt recorded his feelings and moods in a series of deeply felt self-portraits, which are among his finest works.

Dates

1606 born in Leiden, Holland
1624 trains with Pieter Lastman in Amsterdam
1625 sets up studio in Leiden
1631 moves to Amsterdam
1632 paints the *Anatomy Lesson of Dr Tulp*
1634 marries Saskia van Uylenborch
1669 dies in Amsterdam

Katsushika *Hokusai*

Master artist of 'the floating world'

The Japanese artist Katsushika Hokusai is one of the most original and inventive print-makers in the history of art. His bold designs, printed from woodblocks, became very popular in Europe, especially in Paris, and his work had an important influence on the Impressionist painters of the mid-nineteenth century. Hokusai is best known for his *Mangwa* sketchbooks and his *Thirty-six views of Mount Fuji*.

Hokusai was born in Tokyo in 1760. He worked in a bookseller's shop before being apprenticed to a wood engraver. In those days wood engraving was widely used in Japan to reproduce brush drawing, and fine handwriting, called calligraphy, for book illustration. Hokusai soon began designing his own illustrations, and in 1777 he was accepted as a pupil by Katsukawa Shunshō, an artist of the *ukiyo-e* school of painters.

The *ukiyo-e* or 'floating world' artists specialized in everyday subjects of people at work and play, and scenes from nature. Their prints were used to illustrate books or were hung on walls or pasted on to screens. As many as twelve wood blocks might be engraved to print the colours for a single design.

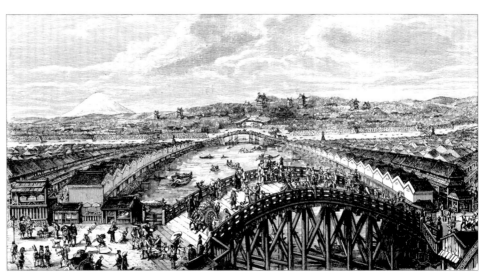

The busy streets of Tokyo, with snow-capped Mount Fuji in the distance, provided Hokusai with subjects to illustrate throughout his life.

Left The
Carpenter's Yard
from the Thirty-
Six Views of Mt
Fuji *series of
prints.*

Hokusai spent two years working for Shunshō, learning *ukiyo-e* printing techniques and studying the art of book illustration. To begin with he found it hard to make a living and was sometimes reduced to selling illustrated calendars on the streets of Tokyo. Soon his reputation grew and he found work illustrating books and greetings cards, which were then very fashionable among the rich.

By the late 1790s, Hokusai was teaching art, and his illustrations appeared in books of poetry, plays and comic writing. He was respected as a gifted artist, although he was an eccentric, lonely man, often scruffily dressed.

In 1814, Hokusai published the first of fifteen books of prints called the *Mangwa*. Every page was filled with pictures recording the street life of Tokyo. Workers, acrobats, animals, birds and fish mingle with figures from Japanese history and legend. After 1820 he worked on a series of colour prints of landscapes and bird and flower subjects. The most famous of these, *Thirty-six views of Mount Fuji*, shows Hokusai's most distinctive style. His theme was Mount Fujiyama, the dramatic cone-shaped volcano near Tokyo, and he painted it as a simple shape, with bold, bright colours. He showed clouds, trees, snow and waves as bold, decorative forms. You can see

Right The Great
Wave of
Kawazama, *one
of Hokusai's most
famous prints.*

20

this in the famous print of the *Great Wave off Kawazama* (below), where Mount Fuji appears beyond the curling wave and spray. The *Mount Fuji* series was reprinted many times and other series, including *Waterfalls* and *Bridges*, followed.

In 1839, many of Hokusai's paintings and drawings were destroyed in a fire, and it is his later works which have survived, showing the strong yet delicate quality of his brushwork. He produced a huge amount of work throughout his life, and is said to have made about 30,000 designs before he died, at the age of eighty-nine.

In the years that followed, Japanese woodblock prints became very fashionable in the West, and the bold, distinctive designs of Hokusai's prints were an important influence on the Impressionist painters (see pages 26-36).

Dates

1760 born in Tokyo
1777 apprenticed to the *ukiyo-e* artist Shunshō
1814 publishes first of the *Mangwa* books of prints
1823-31 produces *Thirty-six Views of Mount Fuji*
1839 many of his paintings and drawings destroyed in a fire
1849 dies

Joseph Mallord William *Turner*

Master of 'coloured light'

J.M.W. Turner was one of the greatest of English artists. He began by painting watercolour views, and soon became interested in capturing the effects of light, weather and atmosphere. His huge oil paintings were often grand classical landscapes influenced by the Old Masters, but he also produced beautiful sketches in oil and watercolour, showing the effects of mist or stormy weather, and the sun at dawn and sunset.

Turner was born in 1775, the son of a barber who lived in London's Covent Garden. As a boy, he coloured prints which were on sale in his father's shop. When he was fourteen, he became a pupil of Thomas Malton, a fashionable watercolour artist whose views of country houses, picturesque ruins and famous buildings were very popular. The same year, Turner entered the Royal Academy School in London, to study art.

Turner pictured sketching in the countryside.

In about 1794 Turner began spending the winter evenings working for an art collector who employed him, with another English artist Thomas Girtin and others, to copy drawings at his academy in the Adelphi Buildings, beside the River Thames. Turner soon became interested in capturing the effects of light, weather and atmosphere in watercolours.

In 1796 Turner exhibited his first oil painting, *Fishermen at Sea,* at the Royal Academy art gallery in London. This success inspired him to produce a series of large oil paintings showing stormy seascapes and dramatic landscapes.

In 1802 Turner travelled to France and Switzerland, studying works of art in Paris and filling sketchbooks with watercolour views of the Alps. After his return to England

Windsor Castle. *Turner painted many views of the River Thames, such as this watercolour showing the castle rising above the river.*

he began work on a series of engravings, showing every type of landscape. Turner wanted people to enjoy pictures of landscapes as much as they did pictures of historical subjects and stories from the Bible. His *Snowstorm: Hannibal Crossing the Alps*, painted in 1812, was based on a story from Roman history, but was also inspired by a dramatic storm he had experienced when out sketching in Yorkshire.

In 1819 Turner made the first of several trips to Italy, filling his sketchbooks with views of the Alps, Venice and the Italian countryside. The climate and light of Italy led to a series of fresh, light-filled watercolours, and he began to paint on-the-spot sketches

Rain, Steam, Speed – *The Great Western Railway. Turner showed this painting at an exhibition in 1844.*

which he called 'Colour Beginnings'. At the same time, he continued to produce finished pictures for the Royal Academy, painting subjects from Shakespeare, the poet Byron, the Bible, Classical history, and his own experience of places and weather. For the *Snowstorm seen off a Harbour Mouth* of 1842, Turner is believed to have had himself tied to a ship's mast for four hours so that he could observe the storm!

Increasingly, Turner experimented with swirling colour, following an idea that colours reflected mood. Critics thought of him as eccentric, not least for the way he made last minute changes to his pictures, painting them as they hung on the walls of the Royal Academy just before an exhibition opened!

Turner's later paintings, especially his watercolours, are spontaneous and free, in some respects similar to the work of much later artists. There is a story that he once advised a pupil to throw a carefully finished watercolour into a jug of water! He continued working right up to his death, at his home in Chelsea, London, painting such 'modern' subjects as steamers at sea and railway trains.

Turner is pictured here putting the finishing touches to one of his paintings in the Royal Academy exhibition.

Dates

1775 born in Covent Garden, London
1796 *Fishermen at Sea* exhibited at the Royal Academy
1802 first tour abroad, visiting France and Switzerland
1819 visits Italy
1828,33,40 returns to Italy
1851 dies in London

Claude *Monet*

Leading Impressionist

Monet is probably the most famous of the Impressionist artists and it was his *Impression: Sunrise*, painted at Le Havre, which gave the group their name. He was fascinated by light and was able to capture fleeting effects of atmosphere and light with short, rapid brushstrokes of pure, strong colour. In later life Monet moved to Giverny, beside the River Seine, where he created a lily pond in the garden. He painted the pond and the garden many times.

Claude Monet was born in Paris in 1840, the elder son of a grocer. He spent his childhood on the Channel coast at Le Havre, where as a teenager he enjoyed drawing caricature portraits. The landscape painter Eugene Boudin, who saw them on sale in the local art shop, was impressed by Monet's drawings, and he encouraged the boy to take up landscape painting in the open air.

On Boudin's advice, Monet visited Paris in 1859, where he met Camille Pissarro, who was studying landscape painting. Monet was then sent to Algeria, in North Africa, for a

Claude Monet in the garden he created at Giverny. He moved to Giverny in his forties, and lived there until the end of his life.

year's military service. When he returned to Le Havre he again began painting out of doors, with Boudin and the Dutch painter Johan Jongkind.

Monet's Impression: Sunrise, the painting which gave the Impressionist movement its name.

In 1862 Monet moved to Paris and enrolled at a studio where he met fellow artists Auguste Renoir, Alfred Sisley and Frédéric Bazille, painting with them in the forest of Fontainebleau outside Paris. His *Woman in a Green Dress* was a success at the Paris Salon of 1866, but the following year his large picture *Women in the Garden*, painted mainly in the open air, was turned down.

Monet became fascinated with capturing the fleeting effects of light and colour in landscape, painting rapidly and directly on to his canvases. He made regular sketching trips with Renoir to La Grenouillère, a popular bathing and boating resort on the River Seine, where he used rapid touches of pure colour to capture the effect of light on the water.

In 1870, after the outbreak of the Franco-Prussian War (1870-71), Monet travelled to London, where he painted views of the River Thames and the city parks. On his return to France the following year, he settled with his wife Camille, in Argenteuil on the Seine near Paris. He continued to paint in the open air, sketching views of the Seine from a boat, often in the company of Renoir and Édouard Manet.

In 1874, after repeated rejections by the Paris Salon, Monet and his friends decided to put on their own independent exhibition in Paris. It was Monet's painting of the harbour at Le Havre, called *Impression: Sunrise*, that led to critics calling the artists 'impressionists', because their paintings looked sketchy and unfinished when compared with the work of other popular artists of the time.

During the 1870s, Monet continued to paint rapid impressions of the landscape, using soft brush strokes and bold colour. He was developing a technique of suggesting forms, using soft touches of varied colour rather than with the traditional use of light and dark tones. In 1883 he moved to a house at the village of Giverny, south of Paris. From here,

Monet's water garden at Giverny.

he made regular painting tours, to the coast of Normandy and Brittany, and to the south of France, recording effects of light and weather.

After 1890 Monet began painting his series of several studies of the same subject, seen at different times of day and in different light and weather. He made fifteen studies of haystacks, using their simple shapes to record the rich colours and glowing effects of different light. He also painted a series of poplar

Monet called this painting Harmony in Blue and Violet. *It is part of the* Waterlily *series that he painted in his garden at Giverny.*

trees, and more than thirty studies of Rouen Cathedral, from different angles and at different hours of the day, to catch the changing light and shade.

In 1893 Monet began to create a water-lily pond in his garden at Giverny. The water-lilies became the subject for a series of increasingly free and abstract paintings. Finally, he produced a huge continuous mural (wall painting), two metres high, of the water lilies, which has now been installed by the French government in the Orangerie pavilion in Paris.

Throughout his life, until he died at the age of eighty-six, Monet continued to record his impressions of 'the most fleeting effects' of what he saw around him. In his determination to paint what he saw, directly from nature, he was the driving force of the Impressionist movement.

Dates

1840 born in Paris
1867 *Women in the Garden*, painted largely outdoors
1870 visits London
1872 settles at Argenteuil
1874 first Impressionist exhibition
1883 moves to Giverny
1890 begins the series paintings of the same subject
1926 dies at Giverny

Mary *Cassatt*

A woman painter in Paris

Mary Cassatt was born in the USA at a time when it was rare for women to be recognized as professional artists. She trained in the USA and in Europe, and settled in Paris, where she joined the Impressionist group of painters. Her pictures were shown at exhibitions of Impressionist art and she also held one-woman shows in Paris and New York. She was greatly influenced by Japanese prints, which helped to develop her distinctive style.

Mary Cassatt was born in 1844 in Pittsburgh, in the USA. Part of her childhood was spent in Europe, and in 1851 the family settled in Paris, then a lively centre for art. On their return to Pennsylvania, Cassatt enrolled at the Academy of the Fine Arts, where she learned to draw copying Classical sculpture, studied life drawing and made copies from Old Masters.

In 1866 she travelled to Paris to spend the summer studying in the studio of a well-known painter called Charles Chaplin. Living in Paris meant that she could visit galleries

Paris in the 1860s, when Mary Cassatt came to study and later to settle. The city was an important centre of the art world at that time.

and see the work of many great and famous painters, but she found herself more interested in the paintings of modern artists such as Gustave Courbet and Édouard Manet, whose work was being shown at the Paris World Fair. These artists were painting scenes of contemporary life, which Cassatt preferred to the classical and historical subjects painted by most other French artists of the time.

In 1871 Cassatt went to Italy where she studied engraving at the Academy at Parma. She visited as many galleries and museums as she could, studying the work of Italian masters like Correggio, whose soft and natural paintings of the Madonna and Child impressed her.

On leaving Italy, Cassatt decided to settle in Paris, where she met Edgar Degas, whose pastel drawings she admired. He invited her to join the Impressionists and she later said of this time: 'I took leave of conventional art . . . I began to live.'

Cassatt's Woman Bathing *shows how she was influenced by the work of Japanese printmakers such as Hokusai.*

Under the influence of the Impressionist painters, Cassatt's range of colours became lighter and brighter, and she began painting out of doors. Degas introduced her to new sources of inspiration, such as the Japanese woodblock prints which were then fashionable in Paris, and the new art of photography. She was fascinated by the way the Japanese print-makers chose unusual viewpoints, often looking down at their subjects from above or from the side, using the shapes and colours of figures, costumes, objects and background to form decorative

The Boating Party, *painted in 1894, is typical of the gentle family scenes that Cassatt often liked to paint.*

patterns. She also saw how photography, too, could offer new ways of looking at a subject.

In 1879, Cassatt exhibited with the Impressionists. By now, she was developing her own favourite subjects; women at the opera, domestic scenes and paintings of mothers and children. She painted in both oil and soft pastels.

After a second trip to Italy, she began working on woodblock prints, planning an illustrated journal with Degas and Pissarro. Inspired by an exhibition of Japanese prints in Paris, she set up her own etching press, and produced her first set of colour prints. In her later art, she worked increasingly with pastels, using bright colours and soft outlines.

From 1911 Cassatt suffered from poor health and her eyesight began to fail, so that by 1921 she was almost completely blind. She died in Paris five years later.

Dates

1844 born in Pittsburgh, USA
1866 studies in Paris
1871 travels to Italy
1877 meets Degas and joins the Impressionists
1879 exhibits with the Impressionists for the first time
1890 sets up her own etching press
1921 becomes blind
1926 dies in Paris

Vincent *van Gogh*

Tortured genius

Van Gogh produced a huge number of drawings and paintings. His early paintings were dark and gloomy, but when he moved to the South of France, his work became filled with brilliant sunshine, warmth and movement. After some time in a mental hospital, where he continued to paint, he moved back to the north. He shot himself in 1890, in a field outside Paris.

In his lifetime, Vincent van Gogh sold hardly any paintings. Today, his works fetch record prices at sales and are known and reproduced all over the world. He is almost as famous for his troubled life and suicide as for paintings such as his *Sunflowers* or *Irises*.

Van Gogh was born in Holland in 1853, the son of a Dutch clergyman. When he was sixteen years old, he began working in the family firm of Goupil, art dealers based in The Hague. During the 1870s, he worked for the firm in London and Paris, visiting art museums and exhibitions whenever he could.

The Potato Eaters, *painted in 1885, shows van Gogh's early style, before he saw the work of the French Impressionists.*

One of van Gogh's many self-portraits, showing the vibrant colours and brushwork of his later works.

In 1876 he decided to follow in his father's footsteps and train as a priest.

In the winter of 1878 van Gogh was sent as a trainee missionary to work in the mining district of the Borinage region of Belgium. There he lived in extreme poverty and became closely involved with the lives of the miners and their families. It was during this period that he began sketching, taking his subjects from the bleak Borinage landscape of chimneys and coal heaps, and the sad figures of the miners. He wanted to paint ordinary working people, and his early works, like *The Potato Eaters* of 1885, are of simple peasants, painted with thick paint, heavy brushstrokes and in dark, earthy colours.

In 1886 van Gogh decided to join his brother Theo, who was a picture dealer in Paris. Here, he first saw the work of the Impressionists and met some of the artists, including Degas and Pissarro, as well as Toulouse-Lautrec, Paul Gauguin and others. His own paintings became lighter and brighter, and he began to paint café scenes, breezy landscapes and colourful portraits of his friends. Pointillism, a new method of painting using dots and 'points' of colour, which was being developed by Georges Seurat, encouraged van Gogh to experiment with his brushstrokes. He was also influenced by the Japanese woodblock prints then fashionable in Paris, with their domestic subjects, strong designs and bold areas of bright colour.

In 1888 van Gogh moved to Arles, in the south of France, where he lived a simple life, painting out-of-doors in all weathers and even by starlight. Inspired by the light and sunshine of the south, he began to paint in strong vibrant colours, using broad, swirling brushstrokes in thick paint to try to capture the energy and life he sensed in nature.

For a while his fellow artist Paul Gauguin joined him in Arles but their conflicting views on art, and their very different

The garden of the mental asylum at St Remy, where van Gogh stayed in 1889.

Van Gogh's painting of the bridge at Arles. Its bright colours and simple brushstrokes show the influence of the Impressionists.

personalities, led to frequent quarrels and resulted in van Gogh slashing his own left ear in a fit of anger.

By 1889 van Gogh was mentally ill and was admitted to hospital in Arles and later to the mental asylum at St Rémy. He continued to paint, his last works showing a disturbing, violent energy with strong, swirling brushstrokes and vivid colours.

In 1890 he moved north to Auvers, where he was under the care of Dr Gachet, a friend of the Impressionists. Here, at the age of thirty-seven, van Gogh shot himself, dying two days later. Although he sold very few paintings in his lifetime, he left thousands of drawings and paintings, including self-portraits, landscapes, interiors and still lifes. These, like the thousands of letters written to his brother Theo, who supported him throughout his life, express his passionate and troubled personality.

Dates

1853 born in Holland
1878 works as a trainee missionary in the Borinage region of Belgium
1885 paints *The Potato Eaters*
1886 joins his brother Theo in Paris
1888 moves to Arles in the south of France; paints *Sunflowers*
1890 dies after shooting himself

Pablo *Picasso*

Twentieth-century genius

Picasso is the most creative and influential artist of the twentieth century. Born in Spain, he spent most of his life in France, where he developed a new style of art, Cubism, which challenged traditional ideas. He worked with many different materials, producing paintings, etchings, sculptures and ceramics (pottery and porcelain objects). Throughout his long life he brought the same energy and inventiveness to everything he did.

Picasso's skill, inventiveness and energy in painting, sculpture, design and ceramics, made him the most creative and influential artist of the twentieth century.

He was born in Málaga in Spain in 1881. His father was a painter and art teacher, and after the family settled in Barcelona, Picasso studied art at the Academy there, later transferring to the Academy of San Fernando at Madrid.

In 1900 Picasso visited Paris, returning to live there the following year. Here, he was able to study works by artists like van Gogh

Towards the end of his career Picasso became interested in designing and making ceramics.

Les Demoiselles d'Avignon, *painted in 1906-7, shocked many people. This painting, which shows human figures in fragmented forms, marked an important change in style for Picasso.*
© *DACS 1993.*

and Gauguin, as well as earlier masters, including the Spanish painters El Greco and Velasquez. For the next four years, he took his subjects from the streets of Paris, painting children or beggars in the sombre blues that he used in most of his pictures at this time, known as his 'Blue Period'.

In 1904 Picasso rented a studio called *Le Bateau Lavoir*, in what was then an unfashionable area of Paris called Montmartre. This became a centre for artists, poets and art patrons. At this time his colours became warmer, based on pinks and greys – this was known as his 'Rose Period' – and for his subjects he used actors, circus characters and harlequins.

In 1906 Picasso produced *Les Demoiselles d'Avignon* – a painting that showed a dramatic change of style. Influenced by the work of Paul Cézanne, and by the tribal art of Africa, Picasso painted human figures broken up into fragmented, angular forms, as if viewed from several angles at once. The following year he met Georges Braque, and together they invented a new style called Cubism. In this style, the artists combined several views of the subject in broken shapes and flat surfaces of colour, trying to express the idea of a subject rather than one view of it. By 1914 Picasso and Braque were including materials such as canvas, wire, rope and newspaper into collages.

During the First World War (1914-18), Picasso remained in Paris, until he was invited to Italy, to design sets for the famous Ballet Russe. While there, he travelled south, visiting the ruins of the ancient Roman city of Pompeii. The ruins and statues he saw there inspired the monumental figures which he painted through the 1920s.

In 1931 Picasso moved south of Paris and set up a sculpture studio and printing workshop. Certain themes, such as the minotaur and the bullfight, appear again and again in his drawings and etchings. He also experimented with metal sculpture, often using 'found objects' such as bicycle wheels or handlebars to suggest new forms.

During the Spanish Civil War (1933-36) Picasso's sympathies were with the Republicans, who were defending their government against the armies of General Franco. In 1936 he painted a huge war picture, *Guernica*. Using broken shapes and dramatic black and white, this painting expresses the horror of war and especially the bombing of the city of Guernica.

After the war, Picasso lived mainly in the south of France. He worked on designs for ceramics and also produced linocuts and engravings, working energetically until his death in 1973, at the age of ninety-two.

Picasso's sculptures, like this goat, often use materials in surprising and amusing ways.

Dates

1881 born in Málaga, Spain
1901 settles in Paris
1906 paints *Les Demoiselles d'Avignon*
1907 developes Cubism with Braque
1936 paints *Guernica*
1973 dies

Barbara *Hepworth*

Sculptor of natural forms

Barbara Hepworth was one of the most important sculptors of the twentieth century. She believed that the sculptor should respond to the natural properties of materials, whether stone, wood or bronze, rather than control them. She created abstract forms, sometimes pierced with holes and using strings stretched across the openings, to suggest natural forms in the landscape. For the last half of her life she lived in Cornwall, where the landscape inspired many of her works.

Barbara Hepworth was born in 1903 in Wakefield, Yorkshire. The rolling Yorkshire dales with their winding lanes and stone walls, made a lasting impression on her and she later wrote: 'All my early memories are of forms and shapes and textures.'

In 1920 she won a scholarship to Leeds School of Art, where she studied sculpture on the same course as another famous English sculptor, Henry Moore. Hepworth then went on to study at the Royal College of Art in London. Like Moore, she became interested in carving directly into stone or wood, bringing out the natural properties of the material.

The cliffs near St Ives in Cornwall, where Hepworth lived during and after the Second World War (1939-45).

In 1924 Hepworth went to Italy to study for a year, learning to carve at a sculpture studio in Rome. She married sculptor John Skeaping and on their return to England they began to show their work at exhibitions in London.

Hepworth's early works were simple figures, influenced by ancient Egyptian and Greek sculpture. In 1931, she began to create abstract, non-representational forms, piercing holes in stone.

After her first marriage failed, Hepworth married the British artist Ben Nicholson, and during the 1930s they lived in Hampstead, London, surrounded by a group of artist friends. On holidays in France, they met Picasso, Braque and the Dutch painter Piet Mondrian. The work of these artists encouraged Hepworth to develop her style and she began sculpting hollowed forms, using colour on the concave surfaces to suggest water. She sometimes stretched taut strings across hollowed or pierced shapes to represent, as she said, 'the tension she felt between herself, the sea, wind or hills'.

During the Second World War (1939-45) Hepworth and Nicholson moved with their children to the Cornish fishing village of St Ives. Hepworth loved the Cornish landscape with its rugged coastline and brilliant light. Many of her works were directly inspired by her surroundings, such as *Pelagos* (1946) which captures the curve of St Ives Bay and the waves pounding the shore.

In 1949 she bought Trewyn studios, where she was able to work in the garden, with space for larger sculpture. Her work was shown at an exhibition in Venice and later she visited Italy and Greece, where she gained fresh inspiration for her sculpture. She began to work on an increasingly large scale, carving pierced forms, with holes that the viewer could look or climb through, or lie down in. Her sculptures never lost their feeling for natural forms and shapes, such as waves, shells or hills. Hepworth once wrote: 'Sculpture to me is primitive, religious, passionate and magical.' She died in 1975 in a fire at her studio. Today, the studio and garden at St Ives are open as a museum to her life and art.

Barbara Hepworth in the garden of her studio in St Ives.

Dates

1903 born in Wakefield, Yorkshire
1924 studies in Italy
1931 begins carving pierced forms
1939 moves to St Ives, Cornwall
1949 buys Trewyn studios
1975 dies in Cornwall

Andy *Warhol*

Creator of Pop Art

Andy Warhol trained as a commercial artist. He began producing silk screen prints, at first using images taken from newspapers and comic strips, then concentrating on everyday objects such as soup cans and Coca-Cola bottles. His mass-produced images, printed at his studio in New York, challenged traditional views of what art should be. His work captured the spirit of the new Pop Art and he became a cult figure, representing a new generation of artists.

Andy Warhol was born in 1930, in Pittsburgh in the USA. He studied painting and design in Pittsburgh before moving to New York to work as an illustrator and commercial artist. His work was displayed in New York department stores and included in glossy fashion magazines, winning an Art Director's Club medal in 1957.

Working in advertising, Warhol became familiar with different techniques of

Andy Warhol, photographed in 1975.

reproduction, and he was able to experiment with methods of printing. He was especially interested in silk screen printing, and in the 1960s he began using this process to make large, decorative images.

At first, Warhol took subjects from newspapers and comic strips. Then he began to concentrate on everyday objects such as Coca-Cola bottles and Campbell's soup cans. When these works were shown in exhibitions in Los Angeles and New York in 1962 they caused a sensation. Warhol became a cult figure, a rebel who was overturning all the accepted ideas of what art should be. The same year he began producing silk screen prints from photographs of famous people like Marilyn Monroe and Elvis Presley. He used bright, garish colours such as orange and neon pink, which gave his prints a strong, poster-like appeal.

Warhol used plain, everyday images, such as this soup tin, for his silk screen prints. Campbell's Soup Can I, © *Andy Warhol Foundation Inc., 1993.*

Warhol opened a studio in New York, called The Factory, and began mass-producing his silk screen prints of celebrities or events in the news. Sometimes the subjects were disturbing or shocking, such as a car crash.

In 1963 he started to make films. His film *Sleep* showed a man sleeping for six hours, and *Empire* focussed on the Empire State Building in New York from a single viewpoint for eight hours. Warhol commented, 'I like boring things. When you just sit and look out of a window, that's enjoyable. It takes up time. My films are just a way of taking up time.'

In all his work, Warhol challenged the traditional values of art and the artist. His machine-like images captured the spirit of a new 'Pop Art', based on the throwaway materials of modern life in the Western world. He represented a new kind of artist, gaining his fame as much from his looks, dress and comments as from his work. In the New York art world of the 1960s, he became a cult figure, leading the way for a new generation of artists, musicians and personalities made famous by the mass media of newspapers and television. He once said, 'In the future everybody will be world famous for fifteen minutes.'

Dates

1930 born in Pittsburgh, USA
1962 first exhibits his silk screen prints of soup cans and Coca-Cola bottles
1963 makes films
1987 dies in New York

Warhol's Marilyn Monroe *silk screen prints on exhibition in Paris in 1990.*

Glossary

Abstract   In art this refers to an image which does not represent anything else.

Anatomy   The physical structure of the body.

Apprentice   A young person who learns a trade or craft under the direction of a skilled worker.

Asylum   The former name for a mental hospital.

Bankruptcy   Business failure through lack of money.

Bronze   A type of metal made from copper and tin, used for making tools and sculptures. The word also means a statue or object cast in bronze.

Buddhist   A follower of the religion of Buddhism.

Caricature   An exaggerated, sometimes comical, portrait.

Chiaroscuro   'Light-dark' in Italian: the word is used to describe the use of light and shadow in a painting or drawing.

Classical   Relating to the art and literature of ancient Greece and Rome.

Collages   Pictures made from pieces of paper, cloth, photographs and other materials, pasted on to a background.

Counter-Reformation   The Roman Catholic reform movement which followed the Protestant Reformation in the sixteenth and seventeenth centuries.

Dowry   The money, land and possessions a woman brings to her husband in a marriage contract.

Engravings   Prints taken from an engraved (cut) hard surface such as metal, wood or stone.

Etchings   Prints taken from metal or glass on which a design has been made by burning out lines with acid.

Fresco   A way of painting directly on to newly plastered walls.

Harlequin   A type of clown.

Impressionists   A group of artists painting at the end of the nineteenth century in France. They recorded their impressions of light and colour in their work.

Minotaur   A monster with the body of a man and the head of a bull, in ancient Greek mythology.

Old Masters   The great European painters of the sixteenth to eighteenth centuries.

Pastels   Chalky coloured crayons.

Pointillism   (Sometimes called Divisionism.) A style of painting using dots of colour. It was developed by the French artists Georges Seurat and Paul Signac in the nineteenth century.

Renaissance   The word means 'rebirth' and is used to describe the revival of interest in Classical art and learning which began in Italy in the fourteenth century, lasting until the early sixteenth century.

Royal Academy   A society founded in London in 1768 to encourage the teaching of painting, sculpture and design in England.

Seascape   A picture of the sea

Silk screen printing   A method of printing a design in ink or paint through a fine mesh screen.

Technique   The skill or art applied to a particular task.

Wood-block prints   Prints made using different blocks of wood for each colour. The surface surrounding the design is cut away from the blocks and inks are placed on these cut away-designs. Each block is pressed on to paper or cloth to make the print.

Woodcuts   Prints made from designs cut into wood.

Books to read

Discovering Art by Christopher McHugh (Wayland, 1992-3). A series of six titles following themes and discussing the art of many of the artists in this book.

Great Painters by Piero Ventura (Kingfisher, 1986)

Introducing Michelangelo by Robin Richmond (Belitha Press, 1992)

Impressionism by Jude Welton (Dorling Kindersley, 1993)

Lives of the Great Twentieth Century Artists by Edward Lucie-Smith (Guild Publishing, 1986)

Monet by Jude Welton (Dorling Kindersley, 1992)

Through the Eyes of Artists by Wendy and Jack Richardson (Macmillan, 1989-92). A series about different works of art and artists.

For older readers

A Biographical Dictionary of Artists ed. Sir Lawrence Gowing (Macmillan, 1983)

Women Artists by Karen Peterson and J.J. Wilson (The Women's Press, 1978)

Van Gogh by Bruce Bernard (Dorling Kindersley, 1992)

Index

Numbers in **bold** refer to art works

Boudin, Eugene   26, 27
Braque, Georges   39, 4l

Cassatt, Mary   21, 30-32
  enrols in Paris studio   30
  studies engraving in Italy   31
  Woman Bathing   **31**
  The Boating Party   **32**
  exhibits with Impressionists 32
Counter-Reformation   10, 14

Degas, Edgar   3l, 32, 35
Dürer, Albrecht   8-10
  view of Nuremberg   **8**
  apprentice in woodcut
    workshop   9
  travels to Italy   9
  sets up workshop in
    Nuremberg   9
  produces *Apocalypse* woodcuts 9
  self-portrait 9, **9**
  engraving *The Knight, Death and
    the Devil*   **9**
  etching   26, 32

Girtin, Thomas   23
Gogh, Vincent van   21, 33-6
  works with poor people in
    Belgium   34
  The Potato Eaters   33, **33**
  Self-portrait   **34**
  moves to Arles   35
  The Bridge at Arles   **36**
  slashes his ear   36
  commits suicide   36

Hepworth, Barbara   40-42
  studies in England and Italy
    40, 41
  moves to Cornwall   41
  exhibits in Venice   41
Hokusai, Katsushika   19-21
  pupil of Katsukawa Shunshō 19
  produces *Mangwa* prints   20
  paints *Thirty-six Views of Mt
    Fuji*   20
  The Carpenter's Yard   **20**
  Great Wave of Karazama   20, **21**
  paints *Waterfalls and Bridges*   21

Impressionist painters   21, 26,
  27, 31, 32

Japanese print-makers   19-21,
  31, 35

Leonardo da Vinci   4-7
  self-portrait   **4**
  works in Verrochio's workshop
    5
  paints *Ginevra di' Benci*   5
  paints *Adoration of the Kings*   5
  Last Supper fresco   **5**, 6
  Mona Lisa   **6**, 6-7
  scientific drawings   5, 6, **7**

Manet, Édouard   28, 31
Medici, Lorenzo de'   12
Michelangelo Buonarroti   11-14
  works in Ghirlandaio's
    workshop   11
  studies sculpture at school in
    Medici garden   12
  carves *Pietà*   12
  carves *David*   12, **13**
  paints ceiling of Sistine Chapel
    11, 13, **14**
  carves figures for Pope's tomb 14
  paints *Last Judgement* on wall
    of Sistine Chapel   14
  designs roof of St Peter's   14
Monet, Claude   21, 26-9
  paints *Woman in a Green Dress* 27
  sketching trips with Renoir   27
  paints *Impression; Sunrise*   **27**, 28
  moves to Giverny   28
  paints series of same subject 28
  Harmony in Blue and Violet   **29**
  paints mural of lily pond   29
Moore, Henry   40

Northern Renaissance   8

Picasso, Pablo   37-9, 41
  leaves Spain to live in France 37
  his 'Blue Period'   38
  his 'Rose Period'   38
  paints *Les Demoiselles
    d'Avignon*   38, **38**

invents 'Cubism' with Braque
    39
  paints *Guernica*   39
Pissarro, Camille   26, 32, 35
Pointillism   35
Pop Art   43, 44

Rembrandt van Rijn   15-18
  apprenticeship   15
  sets up studio   16
  *Jacob blessing the children of
    Joseph*   **16**
  moves to Amsterdam   17
  paints *Anatomy Lesson of Dr
    Tulp*   17
  paints *Nightwatch*   17
  bankruptcy   17
  self-portraits   15, **17**, 18, **18**
Renoir, Auguste   27
Renaissance   4, 11

Shunshō, Katsukawa   19
silk screen prints   43-5

Turner, J.M.W.   22-6
  exhibits *Fisherman at Sea*   23
  Windsor Castle   **23**
  Rain, Steam, Speed   **24**
  paints views of Alps   24
  visits Italy   24
  paints *Snowstorm seen at a
    Harbour Mouth*   25

ukiyo-e school   19

Verrocchio, Andrea del   5
Vinci, da   (see Leonardo)

woodblock prints   21
Warhol, Andy   43
  works as commercial artist   43
  exhibits prints of Coco-Cola
    bottles and Campbell's soup 44
  Campbell's Soup Can 1   **44**
  becomes cult figure   44, 45
  produces silk screen images
    from photographs   44
  opens studio 'The Factory' in
    New York   44